BIG BOOK OF SMASH HITS 4

Published by
Music Sales Limited
8/9 Frith Street, London W1D 3JB, England

Exclusive Distributors:
Music Sales Limited
Distribution Centre, Newmarket Road,
Bury St. Edmunds, Suffolk IP33 3YB, England.
Music Sales Pty Limited
120 Rothschild Avenue
Rosebery, NSW 2018,
Australia.

Order No. AM967835
ISBN 0-7119-8534-0
This book © Copyright 2003 by Wise Publications

Compiled by Nick Crispin.
Printed and bound in Malta by Interprint Ltd.

Your Guarantee of Quality
As publishers, we strive to produce every book to the highest
commercial standards. Throughout, the printing and binding have
been planned to ensure a sturdy, attractive publication which
should give years of enjoyment. If your copy fails to meet our
high standards, please inform us and we will gladly replace it.

www.musicsales.com

WISE PUBLICATIONS
part of The Music Sales Group

London/New York/Sydney/Paris/Copenhagen/Berlin/Madrid/Tokyo

BIG SUR

Words & Music by Daniel Ryan, Conor Deasy, Ben Carrigan,
Paddy McMahon, Kevin Horan, Tommy Boyce & Bobby Hart

4

FOUR MINUTE WARNING

Words & Music by Mark Owen & Eliot Kennedy

Four min-utes left to go,

Cry,___ laugh,___ feel___ love these high___ mo-ments these___ are___ your___ four___ min-utes. I'm count-ing me down,___ four min-utes a sound___ it's al-ways a rest___ when you're a-round.___

Dm⁷ ... Cmaj⁹

bide your time,

⊕ Coda   Dm   F

D.S. al Coda

time.   3. The   thir - ty se - conds left to go. (Is this the end then?)

C   G   Dm   F

Mes - sage on your__ ste - re - o. (Four min - ute warn - ing.) Ev - 'ry - bo - dy wants to know,

C   G

Repeat ad lib. to fade

(what should we do then?)__ What would you do, what__ would you__ do? Yeah!

FEEL GOOD TIME

Words & Music by Beck, William Orbit & Jay Ferguson

Do do do do do do

Do do do do do do.

Do do___ do_____ do_____ do.

do

Do do___ do_____ do_____ do

do.

Now our time,_____ real good time.___

_____ Now our time,___

GUILTY

Words & Music by Gary Barlow, Eliot Kenney, Tim Woodcock & Duncan James

19

I nev-er want_ to hear the things they got-ta say.___
Don't try to tell__ me how he treats you is-n't bad.___

I've found ev-'ry-thing I__ need.__
I need_ you back in my_ life.___

I nev-er want-ed a-ny
I nev-er want-ed just to

more than I could see.__
be the oth-er guy.__

I on-ly want_ you to be-
I nev-er want_ to live a

- lieve.)
lie.)

If it's wrong to tell__ the truth__ what am

HEY WHATEVER

Words & Music by Wayne Hector, Steve Mac, Kenneth Papenfus & Carl Papenfus

Well I can't con - trol the u -

Don't let the gu - rus and phi - lo - so - phers lead you on._____

Ah._____

D.S. al Coda I

Coda
You're a cham - pion__ of science__ or you just__ some__ fr - eak show's fool__

__ what can - not be proved__ no, no,__ can

29

IGNITION

Words & Music by Robert Kelly

say on the ra - di - o: It's the re - mix to "Ig - ni - tion": hot and fresh out the kit - chen. Ma - ma

roll - ing that bo - dy, got ev - 'ry man in here wish - ing, sip - ping on coke and rum.__ I'm like

"So what? I'm drunk!__ It's the freak - in' week - end, ba - by; I'm a - bout to

have me some fun."__ Bounce, bounce, bounce, bounce, bounce, bounce, bounce.

Bounce, bounce, bounce. Come on. 2. Now it's like have me some fun."

Cris-tal pop-ping in the stretch Na-vi-ga-tor. We got food ev-'ry- where, as if the

par-ty was cat-ered. We got fel-las to my left, hon-eys on my right. We

bring them both to-geth-er, we got drink-ing all_____ night. Then

INNOCENT EYES

Words & Music by Delta Goodrem & Vince Pizzinga

MAYBE TOMORROW

Words & Music by Kelly Jones

1. I've been down and I'm won-de-ring why_ these lit - tle black clouds keep - a walk - ing a - round with
2. I look a - round at a beau - ti - ful life_ I've been the up - per side of down, been the in - side of out but we

MIXED UP WORLD

Words & Music by Sophie Ellis-Bextor, Gregg Alexander & Matthew Rowbottom

I JUST DON'T
WHAT TO DO WITH MYSELF

Words by Hal David
Music by Burt Bacharach

ev - 'ry - thing for two, do - ing ev - 'ry - thing with you;__ and
on - ly__ make me sad, and par - ties make me__ feel as bad,__ 'cause
ev - 'ry - thing for two, and do - ing ev - 'ry - thing with you;__ and

1.

now that__ we're_____ through, I just don't know what__ to do._____
I'm not__ with_____ you. I just don't know what__ to do._____
now that__ we're_____ through, I just don't know what__ to do._____

2. I just don't

2, 3.

Like a sum - mer rose_____ needs the sun and rain,__

I need your sweet love

57

NEVER GONNA LEAVE YOUR SIDE

Words & Music by Daniel Bedingfield

1. I feel like a song without the words, a man without a soul,

a bird without it's wings, a heart without a home.

I feel like a knight without a sword, a sky without the sun,

NOTHING FAILS

Words & Music by Madonna, Jemma Griffiths & Allan Sigsworth

Makes me wan - na pray,___ pray._____
makes me wan - na pray._____

RUBBERNECKIN'

Words & Music by Bunny Warren & Dory Jones

It's called rub-ber-neck-in', ba-by, but that's al-right with me.

RE-OFFENDER

Words & Music by Fran Healy

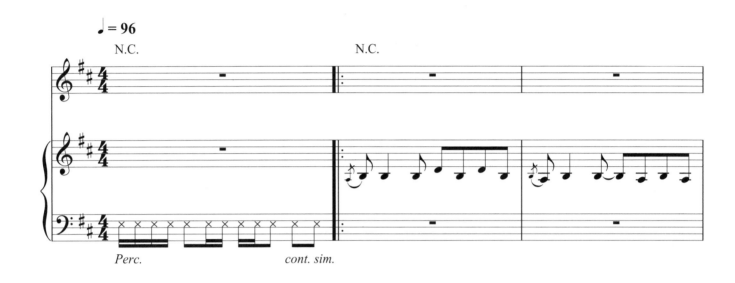

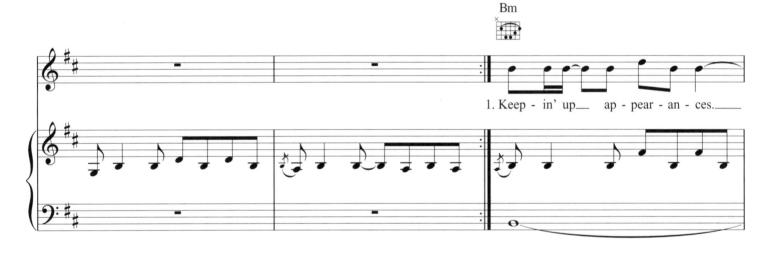

1. Keep - in' up___ ap - pear - an - ces.___

Keep - in' up___ with the Jon - es'.___

THE SCIENTIST

Words & Music by Guy Berryman, Jon Buckland, Will Champion & Chris Martin

1. Come up to meet__ you, tell you I'm sor - ry, you don't know how love-
(Verse 2 see block lyric)

Verse 2:
I was just guessing at numbers and figures
Pulling your puzzles apart.
Questions of science, science and progress
That must speak as loud as my heart.
Tell me you love me, come back and haunt me
Oh, and I rush to the start
Running in circles, chasing our tails
Coming back as we are.

Nobody said it was easy *etc.*

SEXED UP

Words & Music by Robbie Williams & Guy Chambers

SWEET DREAMS MY L.A. EX

Words & Music by Cathy Dennis, Bloodshy & Myron Avant

1. Hey, hang your red gloves up 'cause there's no - thing left to prove now.
2. We've had it on full steam till the light comes back to you now.

Hey, hang your red gloves up, ba - by,
Hey, is it all it seems, is it

Fine

Sweet dreams_ my_ L. A. ex._

Does_ it make you feel a man,_ point - ing the fing - er be-

-cause you can?_ I spell_ it loud_ and clear._

"Ba - by that tongue's not wel - come a - round_ here."_ You turned the ci - ty 'round.

TRAIN ON A TRACK

Words & Music by Robert Fusari, Tiaa Wells, Bale'wa Muhammad & Sylvester Jordan

Train on a track like spokes in - side a wheel, in - vo - lun - ta - ry mo - tion like roll - ing down hill. And there's no way to stop__ it.__ It's a na - tu - ral thing like sun - rise and dusk,

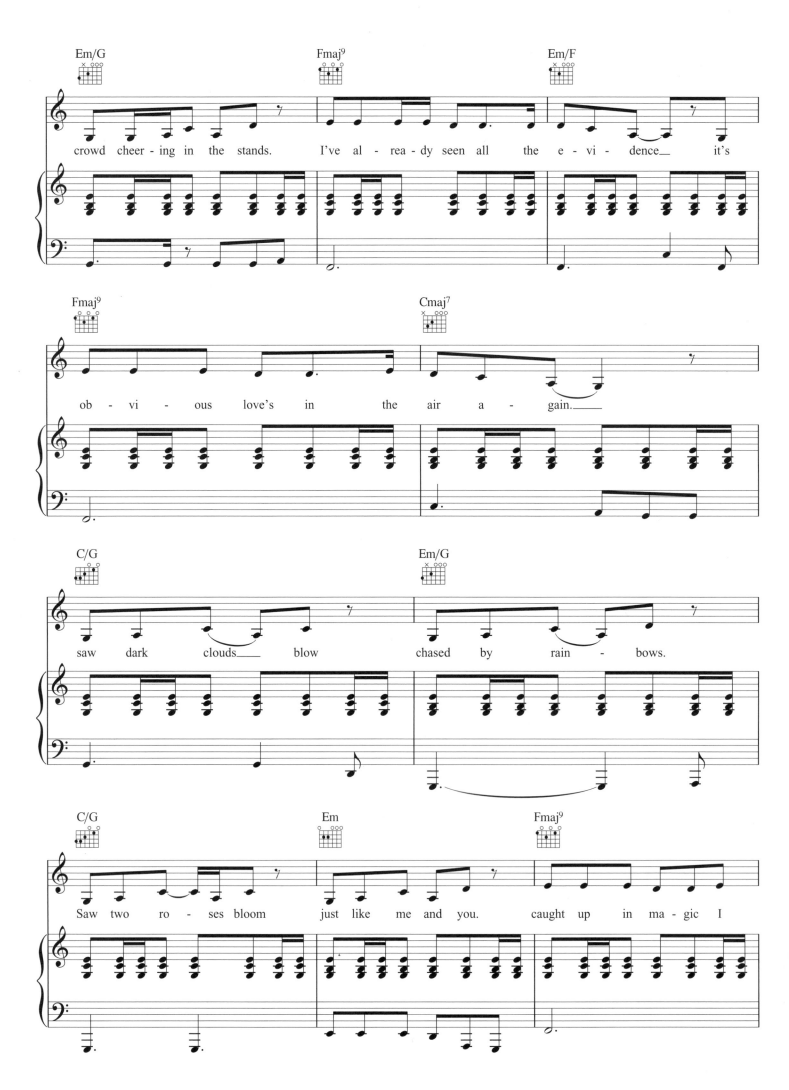

UNDER THE THUMB

Words & Music by Amy Studt, David Eriksen & Karen Poole

we were play-ing games of un-der the thumb, I think you took me for a ride.

1.

What a waste of me. Oh,___ oh,___ oh.___

2.

What a waste of me. Oh,___ oh,___

oh,___ what a waste of me. Oh,___ oh,___

WHAT YOU NEED IS...

Words & Music by Pete Glenister, Sinéad Quinn & Deni Lew

WORLD FILLED WITH LOVE

Words & Music by Craig David & Fraser Smith

WHERE IS THE LOVE?

Words & Music by William Adams, Justin Timberlake, Jaime Gomez,
Allan Apll Pineda, Printz Board, Michael Fratantuno, George Pajon, Jr. & J. Curtis

Verses 1 & 2 (Rap) see block lyrics

(Cri - te - ri - a.)

(Bac - te - ri - a.)

(Ci - ne - ma.)

Where is the love?____ Where is the love?____ Where is the love?____ Where is the love?__

One world, one world.
got…
One world, one world.
That's all we got.

Verse 1:
What's wrong with the world, mama?
People livin' like they ain't got no mamas
I think the whole world's addicted to the drama
Only attracted to things that'll bring the trauma
Overseas, yeah, we tryin' to stop terrorism
But we still got terrorists here livin'
In the USA, the big CIA
The Bloods and the Crips and the KKK.
But if you only have love for your own race
Then you only leave space to discriminate
And to discriminate only generates hate
And when you hate, then you're bound to get irate, yeah.
Badness is what you demonstrate
And that's exactly how anger works and operates
Man, you gonna have love just to set it straight
Take control of your mind and meditate
Let your soul gravitate to the love, y'all.

Verse 2:
It just ain't the same, old ways have changed
New days are strange, is the world insane?
If love and peace is so strong
Why are there pieces of love that don't belong?
Nations droppin' bombs
Chemical gasses fillin' lungs of little ones
With ongoing suffering as the youth die young
So ask yourself, is the lovin' really gone?
So I could ask myself, really what is goin' wrong
In this world that we livin' in?
People keep on givin' in
Makin' wrong decisions, only visions of them dividends
Not respectin' each other, denyin' thy brother
A war is goin' on but the reason's undercover
The truth is kept secret, it's swept under the rug
If you never know the truth, then you never know love
Where's the love, y'all, come on (I don't know)
Where's the truth, y'all, come on (I don't know)
Where's the love, ya'll?

Verse 3:
I feel the weight of the world on my shoulder
As I'm gettin' older, y'all, people gets colder
Most of us only care about money makin'
Selfishness got us followin' the wrong direction
Wrong information always shown by the media
Negative images is the main criteria
Infecting the young minds faster than bacteria
Kids wanna act like what they see in the cinema.
Whatever happened to the values of humanity?
Whatever happened to the fairness in equality?
Instead of spreading love, we spreading animosity
Lack of understanding, leading us away from unity
That's the reason why sometimes I'm feelin' under
That's the reason why sometimes I'm feelin' down
It's no wonder why sometimes I'm feelin' under
Gotta keep my faith alive till love is found
Now ask youself…